Criminal
or
Not

What Is Your Verdict?

By
Samuel A. Francis

SUNSTONE
PRESS

SANTA FE

Sunstone books may be purchased for educational, business, or sales promotional use. For information please write: Special Markets Department, Sunstone Press, P.O. Box 2321, Santa Fe, New Mexico 87504-2321.

Library of Congress Cataloging-in-Publication Data:

Francis, Samuel A., 1936–
    Criminal or not: what is your verdict? / Samuel A. Francis.
      p. cm.
    ISBN: 0-86534-358-6
    1. Negligence, Criminal—United States—Popular works. 2. Criminal liability—United States—Popular works. I. Title.

KF9236.Z9 F73 2002
345.73′04—dc21   2002021240

Published in

SUNSTONE PRESS
Post Office Box 2321
Santa Fe, NM 87504-2321 / USA
(505) 988-4418 / orders only (800) 243-5644
FAX (505) 988-1025
www.sunstonepress.com

Contents

Contents

Introduction

An epidemic is occurring in our justice system in the United States of America and many Americans are unaware of its consequences. Many civil acts of negligence are being classified as criminal acts. Many American citizens who have never possessed any type of criminal intent are being sentenced to prison for acts that since the United States became a country, were not classified as criminal acts. Most citizens in this country face the reality of being charged, convicted and sentenced to prison for behavior that until recently, was not criminal.

"Mens rea," Latin for criminal intent, was the main legal theory upon which most accused people were judged. Today "mens rea" is almost totally ignored.

In our present system there are people who are

convicted of acts that should not be classified as criminal that are sentenced to prison for long periods. These are people who have never possessed any form of criminal intent. If you read the newspapers or watch television you will regularly encounter stories about good impeccable people being sentenced to prison.

I ask the question, why is this happening? The only logical conclusion is that the prosecutors throughout the fifty states have taken it upon themselves to change the criminal justice system. They are the persons responsible for charging people with crimes. They determine whose cases to take to the grand jury for indictment. They are creating crimes out of civil offenses and merely careless acts. The statutes of most states give them the discretion.

This book contains several court cases about people who have been or could become victims of this epidemic. In seven of the ten cases the individuals were formally charged with crimes. In the other three cases the charges were pending. Some of the facts in these stories are real; some are fiction. However, all the people in these stories are fictitious characters. My research allowed me to find three of the jury decisions, the other verdicts were surmised.

I have an opinion whether criminal charges should have been brought in any of these cases. I also know what my verdict would be if I was on any of the juries.

What do you believe and what is your verdict?

1

The Roller Blades Crime

Leslie Miller put on her roller blades, preparing to take her six-month-old baby girl, Donna, on their morning outing. It had been almost a daily event since the baby was four months old.

Leslie's husband, Bob, was an engineer for a large building firm. They got married when Leslie was twenty-seven. That was three years ago. Prior to her marriage Leslie worked as a law clerk in a prestigious law firm. She left the firm just after she became pregnant.

She was an athletic young woman who worked out at a gym regularly. She lifted weights and did all

9

kinds of aerobics, a very athletic young woman with an attractive, strong body.

At seven-thirty a.m. Thursday morning, fifteen minutes after Bob left for work, Leslie finished putting on her roller blades. Donna sat, strapped into her carriage smiling at her mom. Leslie knew her baby loved the morning ride. She pushed her daughter through the open garage and headed for the neighborhood street. The streets she took daily had solid white lines on the curbside that marked the bicycle paths. Leslie got on the street and pushed the carriage along the bicycle path.

About a half hour later she started toward home. She was on a side street and the traffic was light. She pushed the carriage with the traffic, not against the traffic. As she approached the intersection a couple of blocks from her house a vehicle behind her honked its horn. Leslie slowed down and turned her head slightly to proceed with caution. She didn't see a branch in the bike path because her head was turned. When the carriage hit the branch she lost control of the carriage and it flipped into the path of the oncoming vehicle. Leslie fell to the ground. The driver hit his brakes but could not avoid running over the carriage.

Leslie got to her knees as quickly as she could

and crawled to her baby who was still in the carriage at the rear of the vehicle. She unstrapped her child and immediately recognized that her child was dead.

The driver, a man in his early thirties, ran toward her. He had a cell phone in his trembling hand and called for an ambulance. The man remained standing beside Leslie, not knowing what to say.

Leslie cried hysterically as she cuddled her child. About fifteen minutes later the ambulance arrived and also a policeman. The ambulance took Leslie and her child away while the police officer talked to the driver. The driver was not sure why the carriage fell into the path of his vehicle.

The policeman saw the branch in the street and surmised that it had caused the accident. He wrote his report indicating that the branch was the cause and there was no liability on the part of the driver.

When the ambulance arrived at the hospital Leslie was in shock. A nurse had to carefully take the child away from her. The nurse then injected Leslie with a light sedative. Shortly thereafter Leslie became coherent enough to call her husband.

The day after the accident the policeman who had been at the scene arrived at the Miller residence.

He confirmed that the carriage hit the branch and caused Leslie to lose control. The policeman decided that no criminal charges would be filed against anyone.

The following day an article appeared in the daily newspaper describing the accident. No photographs had been taken. Excerpts from the policemen's report were outlined in the article, including a statement that no one would be charged with a crime.

The local district attorney read the article. He couldn't believe that a mother would push a baby carriage in the street, much less using roller blades. He decided to take a look at the law that defined child abuse. He affirmed what he believed. He believed that this mother had acted negligently and without justifiable cause and permitted a child to be placed in situation that endangered the child's life. He decided to investigate the facts of the case.

He arranged for the investigating police officer to meet with him in order to hear the facts first hand. The meeting took about a half hour. The policemen confirmed the facts that the district attorney read in the newspaper. When the meeting ended and the policeman left, the district attorney decided that he would seek a grand jury indictment of Leslie Miller for child abuse resulting in the death of her child.

Approximately one month after the accident the district attorney presented the case to the grand jury. The only witnesses that testified before the grand jury were the driver of the vehicle and the policeman.

The members of the grand jury were reluctant to indict Leslie. However, the district attorney aggressively pursued the indictment. He worked hard attempting to convince the members of the grand jury that they were not convicting Leslie of any crime. All they would accomplish by allowing the indictment was that there was probable cause that a crime had been committed. The members reluctantly agreed to the indictment.

The district attorney knew that Leslie was not a "flight risk" and following the indictment he sent her a copy of the indictment along with a letter informing her that she or her attorney should telephone his office.

Leslie was overwhelmed when she received the documents. She was in tears when she called her husband. He became irate and wanted to call the district attorney. Leslie did her best to calm him. It was decided that she immediately call her ex-boss and seek his help.

Her ex-boss was James Greer. He was a fifty-five year old civil attorney. The firm in which he was a partner consisted of twenty attorneys. The criminal attorney in the firm was Paul Snead, a hard fighting man of fifty years.

James Greer could not believe that the district attorney had Leslie indicted. He did not know the district attorney but he knew of his mean reputation. He told Leslie that his firm would represent her for no charge. He got Paul Snead on the line and they made arrangements for an appointment the next day.

During the next four months various legal maneuvers occurred. The district attorney offered Leslie a plea bargain, no jail time for a guilty plea. Leslie, her husband and attorney agreed to fight the charges.

Motions to dismiss for various legal reasons were unsuccessful. The judge assigned to the case believed there was probable cause that a crime had been committed. The district attorney attacked Leslie aggressively.

Over five months after the death of her child Leslie's trial began. It was a Monday morning in early September.

The proceedings began with the judge reading the indictment to the jury pool. The crux of the charges was that Leslie's pushing of her child in the carriage while wearing roller blades was negligent behavior, and without justifiable cause and it caused her child to be placed in a situation that endangered her child's life.

Twelve jurors were selected along with two alternates. The twelve jurors consisted of seven men and five women. Here are the male jurors. The first male juror was a sixty-one-year-old retired postal employee. He had three adult children. Second was a thirty-nine-year-old engineer who had a ten-year-old son and a seven-year-old daughter. The third was an unmarried twenty-nine-year-old computer programmer. Fourth was a forty-year-old liquor salesman. He was divorced and had three children ranging from six to twelve years of age. Fifth was a sixty-five –year-old retired restaurant owner who had no children. Sixth was an unmarried twenty-two-year-old college student. The seventh was a thirty-three-year-old stockbroker, father of seven-year-old twin girls.

The women jurors were as follows. The first was a thirty-five-year-old housewife, mother of a five-year-old son and an eight-year-old daughter. Next was a sixty-three-year- old retired schoolteacher, mother of two adult children and grandmother of four. Third was a thirty-five-year-old divorced nurse without any children. Fourth was a forty-year-old housewife without any children. The last was an unmarried twenty three-year-old college student.

It was one o'clock when the trial began. The district attorney called the driver of the vehicle that struck the child as his first witness. His testimony lasted approximately an hour and a half. He appeared to convince the jury that he could not avoid the accident.

The investigating police officer was the second and final witness for the prosecution. Much of his testimony was a repeat of what the driver of the vehicle said. He also confirmed that Leslie told him she had pushed her daughter on several occasions while wearing roller skates. He verified the death of the child. His testimony ended around four p.m. The district attorney announced that he had no further witness. The judge adjourned the trial until nine a.m. Tuesday morning.

Promptly at nine a.m. Leslie took the witness stand. Her attorney established that she had an impeccable background. She also testified about her skills on roller blades and that she believed she never had been negligent in the care of her daughter. She cried during most of her testimony.

After her testimony her lawyer called as witnesses several of Leslie's friends and neighbors. They all verified that Leslie was a loving and excellent mother who provided great care for her daughter. All the testimony ended close to twelve noon.

The judge declared a recess until one-thirty.

When the recess was over the attorneys gave their closing arguments. That took an hour. Immediately after the judge gave several instructions to the jury. The following instruction was the focus of the criminal charge against Leslie.

"Leslie Miller has been charged with negligently permitting child abuse resulting in death. For you to find Leslie Miller guilty of child abuse resulting in death, the state must prove to your satisfaction beyond a reasonable doubt each of the following elements of the crime.

1. Leslie Miller permitted Donna Miller to be placed in a situation, which endangered the life or health of Donna Miller.

2. The defendant acted with reckless disregard. To find that Leslie Miller acted with reckless disregard, you must find that Leslie Miller knew or should have known the defendant's actions created a substantial and foreseeable risk, the defendant disregarded the risk and the defendant was wholly indifferent to the consequences of the conduct and to the welfare and safety of Donna Miller.

3. Leslie Miller was the parent of the child.

4. Leslie Miller's actions resulted in the death of Donna Miller.

5. Donna Miller was under the age of eighteen."

After the final instruction was given the jury retired to the jury room to determine her guilt or innocence. It was three p.m.

At five p.m. the jury had not reached a verdict. The judge called them into the courtroom and told them they could go home for the evening and that jury deliberations would begin again a nine a.m., the next day, which would be Wednesday.

The jury renewed deliberations promptly at nine a.m. Wednesday morning. By ten forty-five they reached a verdict.

What is your verdict?

2

Cellular Homicide

In late May the sun was starting to set when Alex Laursen drove his semi truck into Amarillo, Texas. He reached for his cellular telephone and dialed his wife, Linda.

"Hi sweetheart. I'm about ten minutes away from the yard," he said.

"How come you're so late?" she asked.

"A bunch of traffic. Nothing I could do to avoid it."

"I'll jump in the van," she said. "I'll pick you up as soon as I can."

"See you soon," he said, and then hung up.

He drove into the yard, which was on the outskirts of the city, parked his vehicle then went to the office to check out. The clerk greeted him then handed him a large envelope. "What's this?" he asked.

"That's your annual good driving award," she responded. "When's the last time you had a traffic ticket?"

"Around ten years," Alex said with a smile on his face. He waived goodbye, then left the room and went out to meet his wife.

Linda watched Alex approach her vehicle. He looked a little older than his forty years. His five foot ten inch body seemed a little overweight. It looked like he needed to lose about fifteen pounds. He used to be a lot more muscular. Who cares, she thought. I love him.

Alex got in the car and they hugged and kissed. It was close to eight o'clock and Alex was hungry. "Anything to eat at home?" he asked

"Yes," she said. "I saved you some barbecue."

When they arrived home two of his three sons greeted him, seven-year-old Jim and nine-year-old Brian. His third son, twelve-year-old Michael was spending the night at a friend's house.

Two hours later they went to bed. There was a

lot to do on Saturday, soccer, baseball and track.

Most of Saturday Alex spent attending his sons' sporting events. Later in the afternoon he attended a parent teachers meeting at Saint Joseph's Catholic school. The meeting ended around six o'clock. All the family was home by six-thirty. They spent time enjoying each other's company. Linda ordered some pizza for the boys. She and Alex planned to go out for dinner.

Sunday morning the family went to mass. After mass Linda cooked a large Sunday meal. The boys competed for their father's attention. They knew he would be leaving Monday morning for several days. Alex let them stay up late Sunday night so he could spend more time with his family.

Alex was ready to leave the house at six a.m. Monday morning. Linda drove him to the yard. He kissed her goodbye and went to the office to prepare for his trip. Once in the office the clerk gave him his log and his keys. He would be traveling to New Mexico and Colorado. He went to his tractor, started the engine and drove away. It was six-thirty when he left the yard.

Around mid-afternoon Alex drove his vehicle up a steep hill in northern New Mexico. He drove on a state highway that had only two lanes. It was not a divided highway.

The vehicle moved slowly as it reached the top of the steep hill. At the top of the hill he immediately noticed a woman standing beside a Ford Explorer waving her arms at him. He slowly passed her vehicle and then pulled the semi over to the side of the road. He got out of his vehicle and walked over to the woman.

She greeted him and pointed to the rear tire, which was flat. She told him she had no idea how to change a tire. "Could you change the tire for me?" she pleaded.

Alex glanced in the back seat of the Explorer and noticed a small child sitting in a child's chair. It was a girl. "How old is your girl?" he asked.

"She's three and a half."

"How long have you been stranded?" Alex was concerned about the heat damaging the child.

"I pulled over about ten minutes ago." She wondered what Alex was thinking.

"I'll get to work on changing the spare," he said. "But I think you should get the little girl out of the car. She might get dehydrated"

The woman immediately opened the back door and took her child out of the vehicle.

"Do you have any water?" Alex asked.

"No I don't." She shrugged her shoulders. "I'm sorry I'm not prepared for this.

"I've got some in the truck." He went to his vehicle, got a thermos bottle and returned with water for the child. He gave the water to the woman and began to work on changing the spare.

It took him about twenty minutes to finish the job. The woman gave him the bottle and hugged him. "Give the man a kiss," she said to her little girl. The child gave Alex a kiss on the cheek. He smiled.

She reached out her hand and said, "I want to thank you and I don't even know your name. I'm Jenny Wallace and this is Claire." She pointed to her daughter.

Alex took her hand. "I'm Alex Laursen."

"Can I call your boss or something," she said. "I want to tell him how nice of a man you are."

Alex blushed. "Don't worry about that. Now, I need to get going."

She put her child back in her vehicle, said goodbye, got in the vehicle and drove away.

Alex went back to his truck, started it and got back on the highway. It took him a few minutes to get up to the speed limit. He thought about telephoning his wife to tell her what he had just done. He reached for his phone and dialed his wife's number. When he heard the ringing signal on his phone he tucked the phone between his shoulder and his cheek. Just as he thought he heard his wife answer the phone slipped and fell to the floor. He looked down for the phone and reached for the phone with his right hand. His left arm pulled the steering wheel to the left and his truck suddenly went into the wrong lane and hit an oncoming pickup. He got control of his vehicle and was able to avoid another vehicle coming in his direction.

He brought his semi to a stop, got out and ran to the pickup. The pickup was on its side and the driver's side looked like a pancake. He looked at the driver and knew he was dead.

The police were called. They came and did their investigation. Alex told them about stopping to help the woman. He finished the story with the exact truth. They issued no citation to Alex in spite of a man being killed. The police did not feel a crime was committed.

A month passed before an attorney for the deceased's family contacted Alex's employer. Alex knew he committed a civil act of negligence and that the company's insurance company would have to pay.

The district attorney in the district where the

accident occurred always received accident reports involving a death. He was totally against the use of cellular telephones while driving a motor vehicle. The use of cellular telephones in the small town in which he lived was not like in the big cities. He believed that a crime of *Homicide by vehicle* had been committed. The state statute read: "Homicide by vehicle is the killing of a human being in the unlawful operation of a motor vehicle." He took the case to the local grand jury and Alex was indicted. The district attorney convinced the grand jury that Alex drove in a reckless manner when he used his cellular telephone under the facts presented to them. Driving in a reckless manner is one of the main elements required by the statute.

Alex received a letter from the district attorney's office that contained a copy of the indictment and a notice of the time and date he must appear for arraignment. Alex, normally an emotionally strong man, broke down when he realized what was happening.
His entire family was devastated.

Alex's employer was sympathetic but could not offer much assistance. Alex would have to obtain and pay for his own lawyer. He contacted a criminal attorney that had been recommended to him. The attorney quoted him an attorney fee of fifty thousand dollars.

Alex did not have the money. He had enough equity in his home so he borrowed the money to pay the fee.

The trial took place on the second week of September in small town in northern New Mexico. The jury consisted of the following twelve individuals. A forty-seven-year- old automobile mechanic who did not use a cell phone. A sixty-five-year-old retired hospital janitor who never owned a cell phone. A twenty-nine-year-old new car salesman who owned a cell phone. A thirty-five-year-old male high school basketball coach who had just acquired a cell phone. A sixty-eight-year-old farmer who did not own a cell phone. A thirty-five-year-old male loan officer at a bank who had a cell phone. A forty-year-old male bartender who never owned a cell phone. A thirty-year-old female grade school teacher who did not own a cell phone. A sixty-two-year-old housewife, married to a retired truck driver who did not use a cell phone. A twenty-six-year-old female grocery store clerk who owned a cell phone. A fifty-one-year-old female secretary for a Baptist Church who owned a cell phone. A forty-eight-year-old housewife married to a restaurant owner. She owned a cell phone.

The trial began on a Monday morning at nine a.m. It lasted until Wednesday noon. Wednesday afternoon the attorneys gave closing arguments. The prosecution argued that the defendant operated his vehicle in a manner that was likely to endanger any person. Alex's attorney responded that Alex's behavior was an act of civil negligence and not a criminal act.

After the attorneys finished the judge gave instructions to the jury. The two following instructions were the most critical in the case.

First instruction, "For you to find the defendant guilty of causing death by vehicle, the state must prove to your satisfaction beyond a reasonable doubt each of the following elements of the crime:

1. The defendant operated a motor vehicle in a reckless manner;

2. The defendant thereby caused the death of Manuel Salas."

Second instruction, "For you to find that the defendant operated a motor vehicle in a reckless manner, you must find that the defendant drove with willful disregard of the safety of others and at a speed or in a manner that endangered or was likely to endanger any person."

It was close to four-thirty when the judge finished. He decided to let the jury go home for the evening and to begin deliberations at nine o'clock the next morning.

The crime Alex is accused of is a third degree felony. If he is found guilty he could be sentenced to a maximum of six years in prison.

By the end of the day the jury reached a verdict.

What is your verdict?

3

Prison For Owner of Dogs

The Ryans, John, forty-one-years of age and Ursula forty-years-old had been married for twelve years. They met in Germany during John's service in the military. Ursula was born in Germany. They had two children, twelve-year-old John Jr. and nine-year-old Katie. They lived in a small city in the southwest part of the United States in a suburb near the outskirts of the city. The house sat on three-quarters of an acre with a high fence surrounding the back yard.

John worked as a mechanic for a Chevrolet dealership and Ursula did some laundering and ironing for people in the neighborhood. They had two Rotweiller dogs, a five-year-old male and a four-year-old female. They were kept in the backyard which they believed was so secure that the dogs could not ever get out without someone allowing them to do so. In the five years they possessed the dogs they never got out of the yard unless they were accompanied by an adult and on a leash.

Every morning after the children went off to school, Ursula would put a leash on each animal, open the backyard gate and take them for a walk. As she strolled along the sidewalk Ursula encountered many of her neighbors who walked around the neighborhood. Most of the neighbors believed the dogs were tame and very often stopped to pet them. The dogs only got hostile when they confronted other dogs. Ursula used her strong arms to control her dogs around the other dogs.

There were many children of all ages in the neighborhood. Ursula's children played with many of them. On weekends they exchanged slumber nights. Some nights the Ryan children spent a night at their friends and other nights the Ryans had some children spend the night with them. The children who spent the night with the Ryans all raved about Mrs. Ryan's German meals.

The dogs were never a problem to any of the

visiting children. They often went out in the back yard and played with dogs. Occasionally John Jr. and his guests would take the dogs for a walk.

There was a school bus stop on the corner of the block where the Ryans lived. It was a few yards away from their house. One morning in early October as Ursula was leaving to drive her children to school she noticed two neighborhood boys waiting for the school bus. They were two brothers who lived down the street. There ages were nine and six years. She waved at them as she drove away.

Within a few minutes after she left, one of the dogs leaned on the wooden yard gate and it opened. Both dogs moved out of the back yard and slowly sniffed their way to the front of the house. When they reached the front yard they were not too far from the two boys waiting for the bus.

The two boys saw the dogs. The older boy was familiar with the dogs and was not afraid of them. The six-year-old immediately became afraid and started to back away. Suddenly he began to run. This breed of dog has a tendency to chase and attack humans who run. The dogs perked and then began to chase the boy. They caught him easily, attacked him and did not stop until the boy was dead.

The twelve-year-old stood watching in shock.

A man in his home across the street glanced out of his window and saw the dogs sniffing the boy. He was not sure what had happened. He immediately went to his garage, grabbed a baseball bat and ran toward the dogs. When he got within a few yards of the animals they took off running toward the Ryan's house. They ran into the back yard.

The man looked at the mangled child and knew he was dead. He went to the twelve-year-old because he feared the dogs might return. He took the boy back to his house and called 911.

Not long after that, Ursula turned the corner near her home and saw two police cars and an ambulance. She wondered what had happened so close to her home. She pulled in to her driveway, got out of her car and went to the scene. The ambulance drove away and then she recognized the man talking to the police. As she got close the man looked at her and pointed his finger. "That's her, that's the owner." Ursula did not know what that man meant.

The police officer approached her and asked her if she owned two black dogs.

"Yes, I do," she said.

The officer shook his head. "Well, they just attacked and killed a six-year-old boy."

"What," Ursula said. "They couldn't. They're locked in the back yard."

She turned and ran to her house. She saw the open gate and almost fell to her knees. Then she began to cry.

An hour later two people from the city dog pound arrived. They had been ordered to take the dogs. The plan was to destroy the animals according to state law.

Within thirty days Ursula was indicted for the crime of negligent homicide. The law read, " Any person who causes the death of another person by conduct amounting to criminal negligence commits criminally negligent homicide." Her husband was not charged because the district attorney felt that she was the person in control of the dogs.

The criminal attorney the Ryans retained told Ursula that no jury would convict her of this felony, which was a class five felony. The penalty if convicted was a minimum of one year in prison and a maximum of three years.

The case went to trial in mid-January.

The jury consisted of seven women and five men. Juror number one, a thirty- three-year-old female medical student who did not own a dog; juror number two a forty-five-year-old female cocktail waitress who owned miniature poodle; juror number three a sixty-seven-year-old grandmother who owned a cat; juror number four a fifty-year-old female administrative secretary who owned a Chihuahua; juror number five a thirty-eight-year-old liquor saleslady who did not own a dog; juror number six a forty-five-year- old apartment manager that did not allow dogs in the apartment; juror number seven a thirty-five-year-old female stockbroker who owned a small beagle; juror number eight a fifty-five-year-old male bakery owner who did not own any animal; juror number nine a twenty-six-year-old male bookkeeper who owned a fox terrier; juror number ten a forty-year-old male security guard who did not own any animals; juror number eleven a sixty-two-year-old retired male fireman who owned no animals; juror number twelve a thirty-nine-year-old male computer programmer who owned no animal.

The trial began on a Tuesday morning at nine a.m. At the beginning there were only three witnesses for the prosecution: the neighbor who witnessed the dog attack, one of the police officers that arrived at the scene and the coroner for the state.

Each of the five witnesses for the defense were Ursula's neighbors. They all testified that the animals were never aggressive towards humans. Ursula testified on her behalf. During her testimony her attorney showed videos of both dogs playing with the Ryan children and some of their friends. The videos were taken in the Ryan's house and their back yard. These videos made the dogs appear very gentle.

When the dogs were taken to the city dog pound they were frightened and struggled with the employees who treated them harshly. Muzzles were placed on the dogs and this made them very aggressive. One of the handlers took videos of the dogs, which made them appear vicious. In his rebuttal testimony the district attorney showed these videos to the jury. These videos strongly countered the videos shown by Ursula's attorney.

The trial ended late Thursday. Friday morning at nine a.m. would be the time for closing arguments.

Promptly at nine o'clock the district attorney began his closing argument. He argued that Ursula was criminally negligent because she should have been aware that a risk existed for these dogs to attack a human if left unguarded. He argued that the dogs were tame only when Ursula was around. He also argued that they were vicious when she was not present as was shown by the videos taken at the pound. She was negligent by not making sure the dogs could not leave the yard without her.

Her attorney argued that Ursula could not have perceived any risk that her dogs would attack any human. The entire time she owned them they had never been aggressive to any person, young or old. He went over the testimony of the neighbors who verified Ursula's testimony. Finally, he tried to convince the jurors that the animals' behavior at the pound was out of fear and not aggression or meanness.

After closing arguments the judge gave several instructions to the jury. He gave the following instruction describing the conduct necessary to be convicted of negligent homicide.

"To be guilty of criminally negligent homicide the defendant must fail to perceive a substantial and unjustifiable risk that a certain result will occur and the risk must be of such a nature that the defendant's failure to perceive it constitutes a gross deviation from the standard of care that a reasonable person would exercise under all the circumstances."

The crime of criminally negligent homicide is a fifth degree felony, which requires a guilty person to serve in prison a minimum of one year and a maximum of four years.

At eleven o'clock the judge finished with the instructions. He sent the jury to the jury room to elect a foreman and begin deliberations.

The jury deliberated until twelve o'clock and then left for lunch. They returned at one-thirty and commenced their deliberations. Two hours later the foreman informed the judge they had reached a verdict.

What is your verdict?

4

A Medical Act of Criminal Negligence

Julie Woods worked as a nurse on the late shift at a hospital. Her starting time was ten p.m. and ended at eight a. m. three nights a week. She got off in time to go home and see her husband off to work.

He worked as an accountant in a small accounting firm. He drove their seven-year-old daughter to school three days a week. The school bus brought her home and Julie slept until the daughter arrived.

She loved being off work for four days so she could spend most of her spare time with her daughter. Julie was as conscientious as a parent as she was a nurse. She also devoted much of her spare time to her husband.

Julie had worked as a nurse for the last eight years, since she was twenty-seven. She married her husband the same year she began working. For the last two years she received an award as nurse of the year for her hospital. She loved her work. Her belief in her work was that she should treat every patient as though they were members of her family. It was not unusual for patients to comment to the hospital or write to the hospital saying that Julie made them feel like a family member.

On a Tuesday night in late July Julie entered quietly into her seven-year-old girl's bedroom to kiss her goodbye. She did this each of the nights she went to work. She then went to her husband, gave him a hug and then drove to work.

It was nine forty-five when she arrived at the hospital. She followed her normal procedure and began her night's work. At three a.m. Terri Robins, a thirteen-year-old girl was brought into Julie's ward from the emergency area of the hospital. Her parents accompanied her. The girl had been involved in an automobile accident, suffered some broken bones and was in extreme pain. Terri obtained the girl's records and examined them. She saw the girl had been given a heavy dose of morphine and would require another around seven o'clock.

The girl's parents asked Julie to make sure the girl's pain would be taken care of. Julie assured them that she would take good care of their daughter. After talking to the parents for a few moments Julie became aware that they were wealthy people. A half-hour later the parents left.

At seven a.m. Julie reviewed the doctor's orders that indicated a dosage of morphine to be given to Terri. In an hour she would be off work. She felt very tired. She did not notice a decimal point in the number of milligrams of morphine required by the doctor. She injected the girl with an overdose of morphine.

At eight o'clock Julie left the hospital. Fifteen minutes later the nurse that replaced Julie went to examine Terri. She found that Terri was not breathing. Emergency measures were taken to attempt to revive her. They did not succeed. Terri was pronounced dead.

The doctor on call examined Julie's notes and recognized that she gave an overdose of morphine to the girl. He immediately called Julie and gave her the bad news.

Julie was reading the newspaper when the doctor called. The information he gave her shocked her.

She put on her clothes and rushed to the hospital. When she got there she obtained the doctor's order, read the morphine requirement and realized she made the mistake. She broke down and cried.

Several weeks later Terri's parents made an appointment with the district attorney. They wanted someone prosecuted for the death of their child. Before attending the meeting they consulted with a criminal attorney. He told them no one had ever been charged with a crime for an incident like this. The only possible crime was criminal negligence. He recommended that they not pursue a criminal indictment. They did not accept his advice. Instead, they studied the criminal negligence statute and believed it did apply in this case.

The district attorney knew the background of Mr. and Mrs. Robins. He knew the purpose of their meeting with him. He did not prepare for the demands this wealthy couple would make.

Shortly after the meeting began the Robins presented the district attorney with a copy of the negligent homicide statute. They watched while he read the statute. When he finished they demanded that either the doctor or the nurse be prosecuted for negligent homicide.

The district attorney told them the same thing

that their criminal lawyer had told them. "No one has ever been prosecuted for a crime in circumstances like this."

Mrs. Robins responded. "Just because in the past society has permitted these people to kill someone and not get prosecuted does not make it right. Someone needs to pay for our daughter's death. The negligent homicide statute requires that they be prosecuted."

After an hours meeting the district attorney assured the Robins that he would take the case to the grand jury. They advised him they wanted to be in the courthouse the day he presented the case. He told them they would be notified.

Two weeks after the meeting the district attorney got ready to take the case to the grand jury. He decided that probable cause existed that a crime may have been committed and that a jury trial was justified. The Robins were at the courthouse when he presented the case to the grand jury. They were not allowed in the grand jury room.

It took two hours for the district attorney to present his case to the grand jury. He had the doctor from the hospital as his main witness. The doctor confirmed that the overdose killed the girl and that the nurse's mistake caused the death of the girl.

After a lot of dissention the grand jury made its decision. The district attorney left the room and approached the Robins who stood in the hallway. "The grand jury has returned a true bill. That means that the nurse, Julie Woods, has been indicted for negligent homicide for the death of your daughter."

The Robins were content. They thanked him for his efforts and left.

Five days later Julie received a notice of the grand jury indictment. The notice informed her that she must be present for an arraignment in one week. She was so distraught she decided to take off work for several days.

She telephoned her husband and told him about the indictment. He felt anger against the system and sorrow for Julie.

The day after Julie received the notice an article appeared in the local newspaper describing the facts of the indictment. The article criticized the idea that an act of civil negligence would be tried as a negligent homicide.

An article appeared in the local newspaper on the front page reporting the indictment. The indictment created a lot of controversy in the community. Criminal attornies throughout the city became outraged by such a charge. The first attorney Julie contacted quoted her a fee of fifty thousand dollars, but because of his personal stand against such an indictment he offered to reduce the fee by one-half. Before Julie agreed to pay the attorney, one of her friends suggested she talk to another attorney who was considered to be one of the best criminal attorneys in the area.

Julie met with the attorney and to her surprise he offered to take her case and he would not charge her a fee. He told her that he believed no jury would convict her of any crime based upon the facts of the case. She felt glad that she would not have to pay anything and also felt comfortable with his confidence.

Subsequent to the arraignment, where Julie pleaded not guilty, her attorney made several attempts to get the indictment dismissed based on legal theories. On occasion it appeared the judge might agree but in the end the judge would not dismiss. The attorney felt that the parents of the deceased child had some influence in the case.

The trial began in mid-February. The number of people in the jury pool was exceptionally large because the judge knew it would be difficult to find people who had not heard of the case. It would be difficult to find jurors that had not already made up their minds.

For an average case it took about a half day to pick a jury. This case took two full days. The prosecutor did all he could to keep anyone from the medical profession off the jury. But in the end it appeared the judge found the necessary unbiased jurors, six women and six men.

The first juror was a forty-three-year-old female stockbroker. She was single and did not have any children. The second juror was a fifty-five-year-old male accountant, married, with a sixteen-year old daughter. Juror number three was a sixty-one-year-old male postal employee, married with four adult children. Juror number four was a twenty-nine-year-old male manager of a Burger King Restaurant. He was divorced and had no children. The fifth juror was a twenty-eight-year-old male plumber, married with two children, a four-year-old daughter and a two-year-old son. Juror number six was a thirty-eight-year-old female office manager, married with one child, an eleven-year-old boy. Juror number seven was a forty-five-year-old male pharmacist, married with three children, two daughters thirteen and eleven and a son seven-years-old. The eighth juror was a sixty-two-year-old housewife with three adult children. Juror number nine was a forty-nine-year-old unmarried male janitor. Juror number ten was a forty-six-year-old female advertising sales woman, married with twin sixteen-year-old boys. Juror number eleven was a twenty-four-year-old unmarried college student. The final juror was a thirty-eight-year-old female college professor, married with a fifteen-year-old son.

The trial began at nine a.m. on the third day. A coroner was called as the prosecutor's first witness. It was not difficult for the prosecutor to prove the cause of death. An overdose of morphine was proven as the cause. The prosecutor knew he needed more evidence to show a crime. He called as his most damaging witness the doctor who wrote the order requiring the morphine to be given to the patient. The doctor had in his possession the document, which showed the number of milligrams prescribed and the decimal point that Julie failed to see. The prosecutions case took a half day.

During cross-examination of the doctor Julie's attorney brought out that on more than one occasion decimal points had been overlooked but no one died from the error. The doctor also made it clear that he knew of no criminal charges being filed against anyone for acts of negligence in the medical profession, which he admitted occurred in this case.

Julie testified on her behalf. She made an excellent witness. She admitted her error and took full responsibility. The jury seemed impressed by her candor. Her attorney believed he could convince the jury not to convict her.

The trial ended around four o'clock that afternoon. Closing arguments were scheduled for the following morning.

Closing arguments began at nine-thirty. The prosecutor attempted to convince the jury that sympathy for Julie should not enter into their decision. He told them a child had been killed and the defendant was the cause. He asked them not to judge this case on the fact that no criminal charge had been brought in the past for this type of negligent act. He argued that Julie knew that a risk existed if any person was given an overdose of morphine. "She failed to perceive that risk and she deviated from the standard of care required by the circumstances."

Julie's attorney argued that she was not a criminal. He told the jury that ordinary medical personnel had made similar errors in the past. She did not deviate from the standards required. He admitted she committed an act of negligence. But, he told them, " That is all it is, an act of negligence not a crime." He argued that finding her guilty of a crime would change the meaning of "crime." He finished at eleven o'clock

Following closing arguments the judge gave the jury instructions. The crucial instruction was the last.

"A person acts with criminal negligence, or is criminally negligent, with respect to circumstances surrounding his conduct or the result of his conduct when he ought to be aware of a substantial and unjustifiable risk that the circumstances exist or the result will occur. The risk must be of such a nature and degree that the failure to perceive it constitutes a gross deviation from the standard of care that an ordinary person would exercise under all the circumstances as viewed from the actor's standpoint."

After the judge gave the final instruction the jury left the courtroom and began deliberation. They did not know that a conviction would require Julie to spend a minimum of one year in prison.

It took the jury until late the following day to reach a verdict.

What is your verdict?

5

Unintentional Injury Or Animal Cruelty

Dale King, his wife and two children moved into their home in a new neighborhood. People with middle class incomes owned most of the homes. Dale was a physicist and worked for the federal government. He was forty-six-years-old. His son was twelve and his daughter was nine.

Shortly after they moved in the family became acquainted with several of their neighbors. Dale attended a group meeting of neighbors organized against crime. He volunteered to serve as block captain. He was the type of man who believed in helping his neighbor.

Dale was not a lover of domestic animals. He did not own any dogs or cats and he would not allow his family to own any. He did not like neighbors' animals coming on his property but never displayed cruelty to any animal.

His next-door neighbor owned two dogs, a large Labrador and a Dachshund. Occasionally the neighbors allowed the dogs to go out on their front yard unsupervised. Sometimes the dogs would go into Dales' yard and relieve themselves. This was offensive to Dale.

One Sunday afternoon Dale noticed the dogs on his property. He immediately went to the dog owner's house. He knocked on the door. The neighbor's wife opened the door and greeted Dale politely.

Dale responded, "I need a favor from you. Your dog has been using my yard as a bathroom and I'd like it stopped." His tone was harsh.

"I'm sorry," she answered. "I'll try not to let it happen again"

"Thank you," Dale said. He quickly walked away.

The woman went to her husband and told him about the conversation with Dale. They agreed not to let the dogs out front without their supervision.

Several weeks passed and Dale forgot about the problem until a Sunday morning in late October when he was in his front yard raking weeds. The Labrador, whose name was Tricks, headed into Dale's yard. Dale had his back toward the dog and did not see the dog. The dog sniffed around for a moment then went toward a bush not too far from Dale. Just as the dog began to squat next to the bush Dale turned and saw the dog. He did not want the dog to poop in his yard so he reached out with the rake. His intent was to tap the dog on the rear and scare him away. The dog suddenly turned his head towards the rake and the prongs struck the dog in both eyes.

The dog began wailing and moving in circles. Dale tried to go to the animal to see the damage but the dog moved to fast for him.

Inside the dog owners' home the woman and her husband were drinking coffee when the wife said, "What's that?" "It sounds like our Tricks," the husband replied.

They jumped up, went to the front door and out to the front yard. What they saw shocked them. The husband ran to the dog, which was now on its own property. He was able to grab it and calm it to some degree. He waved to the wife to come help him. She saw the blood coming from the dog's eyes.

"What have you done to my dog," she yelled at Dale.

Dale walked to them and responded, "It was an accident. I was just going to tap him on his rear and he suddenly turned. I couldn't stop. I'm so sorry."

"I'll bet," the husband responded. No more words were spoken. He lifted his dog and took it inside his house.

Monday evening after Dale got home from work he went next door to ask about the dog.

The husband opened the door and said, "What do you want."

"I just wanted to check on the dog."

"You killed him," the man said, then slammed the door.

One week later, after talking to an attorney, the neighbor and his wife obtained an appointment with the district attorney. They presented him with the facts and requested that Dale be prosecuted for cruelty to animals resulting in death, which was a fourth degree felony. They did not tell the district attorney about Dale's explanation as to what happened.

The district attorney agreed to take the case to the grand jury. He told them they would not be needed to testify at the grand jury proceeding. However, if an indictment were obtained it would be necessary for one of them to testify at a jury trial. They both agreed they would be ready to testify.

Three weeks later the grand jury indicted Dale on one count of extreme cruelty to animals. Following is part of the state's statute defining cruelty to animals.

"E. Extreme cruelty to animals consists of a person:

(1) intentionally or maliciously torturing, mutilating, injuring or poisoning an animal; or

(2) maliciously killing an animal.

F. Whoever commits extreme cruelty to animals is guilty of a fourth degree felony."

The maximum sentence for a fourth degree felony in that state is eighteen months in prison.

Notice of the indictment was mailed to Dale. He could not believe that he could be charged with a criminal act. Maybe civil negligence, but not criminal behavior. His wife was angry that the "system" could create this kind of problem for her husband.

Dale contacted a criminal attorney. After Dale told the attorney the story the attorney found it difficult to believe that an indictment followed such an innocent act. Only one witness to the incident existed and that was Dale. Maybe the district attorney did not know the entire story.

Unfortunately the attorney wanted a twenty-thousand dollar retainer to defend the case through trial.

Once Dale paid the fee the attorney met with the district attorney. The attorney explained the whole incident. After he heard the defense story the district attorney quoted the neighbors who told the district attorney about Dale's behavior when he first complained to them. The district attorney did not believe Dale's story.

Five months later the trial began. Dale's attorney knew that he would have a difficult time finding jurors who did not own a dog or cat. He knew the district attorney would want mostly animal owners on the jury.

Eight women and four men were selected to the jury. The first juror was a thirty-five-year-old female secretary. She owned a five-year-old male beagle. The second juror was a forty-year-old female bartender. She owned two dogs, a two-year-old male poodle and a six-year-old female mutt. The third juror was a fifty-seven-year-old female telephone operator an owner of one dog, a seven-year-old golden retriever. Juror number four was a thirty-three-year-old male postal employee who did not own any animals. Juror number five was a thirty-six-year-old female pharmaceutical representative. She owned no animals. The sixth juror was a forty-nine-year-old male real estate agent. He owned a large eight-year-old German Shepard. Juror number seven was a sixty-six-year- old retired male college professor. He owned no animals. The eighth juror was a twenty-four-year-old female college student. She did not own any animals. Juror number nine was a fifty-nine-year-old housewife who owned a ten-year-old Doberman. Juror number ten was a thirty-eight-year-old male Fed-Ex employee. He did not own any animal. The eleventh juror was a twenty-nine-year-old female hairdresser who owned a six-year-old female English bulldog. The final juror was a twenty-eight-year-old female airline employee. She did not own any animal.

Dale and his attorney felt good that the animal owners represented only half of the jurors.

The trial began at one p.m. At that time the prosecutor called as his first witness the veterinarian who treated the animal then put it to sleep. He testified that the dog was blinded by a sharp instrument and could no longer live. The cause of the killing of the animal had been proven.

The prosecutor called the neighbor's wife as his second and last witness. She testified that Dale came to her house and belligerently told her not to allow her dog to leave her property without a leash. She said he appeared very angry because her dog relieved itself on his property. She felt threatened that Dale might harm her dog and believed that Dale intentionally hurt her pet.

Dale's attorney was aware that the prosecutor proved that Dale's action ultimately caused the dog's death, but he believed Dale could take the stand and convince the jury that the occurrence was an accident. Dale would be the only defense witness.

When Dale took the stand his attorney began asking questions about Dale's background. He had Dale tell the jury about his feelings about dogs. Dale appeared to convince the jury that he did not feel hostile to dogs. Testimony was brought out about the reasons Dale went to his neighbors when the dog used his yard to defecate. Dale told the jury he was not angry when he talked to his neighbor.

His attorney got Dale to emphasize that he did not have any intention to hurt the dog. Dale expressed sorrow because of the death of the dog.

At four-thirty p.m. the trial ended.

During closing arguments the prosecutor attempted to convince the jury that Dale did not tell the truth about the incident. "The defendant should not have used that rake on that animal for any purpose." Those were some of the prosecutor's final words.

Dales' attorney told the jury that Dale was an honest man, a man of integrity. He reminded the jury that the only witness to the event was Dale. No one else should speculate about how the damage occurred. "You must believe the only witness to the accident."

It was six p.m. when closing arguments ended. The judge decided to wait until morning to give the jury instructions. He told the jury to return at eight-thirty the next morning.

At nine a.m. the judge gave the jury the court's instructions. The final instruction was the most critical.

"For you to find the defendant, Dale King, guilty of extreme cruelty to animals as charged in count one, the state must prove to your satisfaction beyond a reasonable doubt each of the following elements of the crime:

1. The defendant caused injury to the dog, Tricks.

2. The defendant acted intentionally and without justification.

At ten o'clock the jury left the courtroom to begin it's deliberations. They reached a verdict at eleven-thirty.

What is your verdict?

6

Inclement Weather Child Abuse

Two years had past since Brad Howard and his wife Jane got a divorce. Jane received custody of their son, Darren, who was eleven-years-old at the time of the divorce. Brad was allowed custody of the child for July and August of each year.

Brad, thirty-nine–years-old was an in-house corporate attorney. He was medium built, handsome with an affinity for good-looking women. This affinity was the main reason for his divorce.

On several occasions his wife discovered him being unfaithful to her. She forgave the first occurrences but in the end she could not forgive and she became very bitter. At the end of their marriage she refused to speak to Brad. She often expressed her hate for him.

Brad belonged to a country club. He loved golf and it was one of his main means of recreation. His handicap was a six. He received five weeks vacation each year. He took those vacation days during the month of August. During those days he played golf almost every day.

The country club provided a junior program for the children of the members. Darren participated in this junior program, which allowed the juniors to play three times a week after three p.m. Darren loved golf almost as much his father.

Each day that his son played Brad remained at the club waiting for him. While waiting Brad either practiced, played cards or enjoyed a cocktail or two. When Darren finished around seven p.m. he and Brad would have dinner together. Brad cooked occasionally and other times they went out for dinner. The father and son enjoyed a very close relationship.

Darren became Jane's focus in life. She didn't like having to allow Brad two months custody. During the time Brad had custody Jane telephoned Darren every evening. When Brad answered the telephone Jane would not be courteous to him.

On a Thursday afternoon in late August Brad teed off at one-thirty p.m. at his country club. He finished at four-thirty, one and a half hours after Darren began his round off golf with three of his friends. When he went into the pro shop he noticed the dark clouds that appeared in the distance. It looked like it might rain.

The club's pro shop contained a lightning sensor. If lightning existed within five miles of the sensor it would become activated and would sound for two minutes. The purpose was to warn the golfers that lightning was in the area. When the lightning went away the siren would sound again so that the players would know the danger had passed.

At five o'clock Brad stood in the pro shop talking to the assistant pro. They talked about the weather when the siren sounded. Brad asked the assistant how close the lightning existed. He did not want Darren exposed to any danger from the lightning.

The assistant responded that the sensor could not tell the distance. It only warned that the lightning existed within a five-mile radius.

Brad walked outside and looked at the clouds. They did not seem to be menacing but he decided to go get Darren and bring him and his friends to the clubhouse. He borrowed a golf cart and drove to hole number eight where he saw Darren and his friends sitting on a bench waiting for the weather to clear.

Brad approached the boys. "There's lightning around. Maybe you guys ought to go in the clubhouse. Wait it out."

"There's been no lightning close by," Darren answered. "It's way off. We're watching."

Brad looked at the sky and saw that there were no dark clouds over the course. He agreed with his son.

"How you playing?" Brad asked.

"Pretty good. I've had two pars."

"Okay. Remember if the clouds get worse, you guys go to the clubhouse."

"We will," Darren replied. "Don't worry."

Brad drove back to the clubhouse, left the cart and went into the card room. He joined the men with whom he just played and ordered a cocktail. He was in the card room for about an hour when he heard a loud thunder. He thought about his son, and then decided to go check on the lightning.

As he walked through the pro shop he glanced out the window and saw a young boy running toward the clubhouse. Brad recognized the boy as one of his son's golf mates.

"What's wrong?" Brad asked.

"Darren's been struck by lightning," the frightened boy responded.

Brad grabbed the boy by the arm and they jumped into a golf cart. The boy led Brad to his son. Darren was lying on the ground unconscious. Brad checked his pulse. None existed. Brad tried not to panic. He picked up his son, put him in the cart and drove to the clubhouse where they called an ambulance that took the two of them to the hospital where Darren was pronounced dead.

Brad telephoned Jane. She went into a stage of shock, crying and screaming. She could not believe that Brad permitted Darren to remain on the course during a lightning storm. She hollered at Brad telling him that he was at fault for not protecting her son.

Several days later Darren was buried. Jane refused to speak to Brad at any time. Brad did not seem concerned about Jane's behavior, but he felt that he could have prevented the incident if only he had taken Darren into the clubhouse. His guilt overwhelmed him.

Two months later Jane's anger had not subsided. She felt that Brad neglected her son and that somehow Brad should be punished. Since she could not punish him, her only choice was to talk to the district attorney and see if Brad could be charged with a crime.

On a Tuesday morning in late November Jane went to an appointment with the local district attorney. She was fifty-years-old and the mother of three children. Jane told her a story of what she found out about the afternoon Darren was killed. A few days after the accident Jane went to the club and discovered the warning system. She also found out that the alarm had sounded and Brad heard the alarm and he failed to act. Jane finished by asking the district attorney if Brad's behavior constituted a criminal offense.

Before answering Jane she consulted the law book that described child abuse or child abandonment. She studied it for several minutes. The clauses that caught her attention read, "Abuse of a child consists of a person knowingly, intentionally or negligently and without justifiable cause causing or permitting a child to be; 1. placed in a situation that may endanger the child's life or health; 2. exposed to the inclemency of the weather." She reached the conclusion that Brad did commit a crime, which was a first-degree felony. She told Jane that she believed Brad committed a crime and that she would present the case to the grand jury. The district attorney also told Jane that the crime was a first-degree felony and that Brad could face up to eighteen years in prison.

Jane left the office satisfied that she did the right thing.

Three weeks later a grand jury indicted Brad on charges that he placed his son in a situation that endangered his life and that he exposed his son to the inclemency of the weather. When he was notified of his indictment he could not believe it was real. He immediately called a friend who was a criminal attorney. Brad took the indictment to the attorney who called the district attorney. She disclosed that Jane was the one who brought the situation to her. She did not blame Jane for causing the indictment. When the attorney told Brad about Jane, Brad broke down.

Brad's attorney attempted to get the district attorney to allow Brad to plead to a misdemeanor charge. The district attorney would only agree to a guilty plea to one felony count with a guarantee of probation. Brad would not accept her offer.

In the second week of April the trial began. Here is a list and a brief description of the jurors who would decide Brad's guilt or innocence. Juror number one was a thirty-two-year-old housewife mother of twin boys who were six-years-old. Juror number two was a forty-nine-year-old female marketing agent for a television studio, married with a twenty-two-year-old son who was an avid golfer. The third juror was a fifty-five-year-old male automobile dealer. He was and avid golfer and had two grown sons that enjoyed golfing. The fourth juror was a twenty-three-year-old male college student who played on the college golf team. Juror number five was a thirty-six-year-old female hairdresser who had a twelve-year-old daughter. Juror number six was a forty-seven-year-old real estate agent, mother of a twenty-year-old son and a nineteen-year-old daughter. She played golf in a real estate golfers league. The seventh juror was a fifty-five-year-old male nurse, single, no children and did not like the game of golf. Juror number eight was a twenty-nine-year-old divorced female cocktail waitress, mother of a five-year-old son. Juror number nine was a sixty-five-year-old retired male structural engineer who played golf regularly. He had five adult children none of whom had ever played golf. The tenth juror was a thirty-two-year-old female pharmacist, not married without golf experience. Juror number eleven was a thirty-eight-year-old male soccer coach who spent a lot of time in the outdoors. The final juror was a fifty-nine-year-old male veterinarian, married with three grown children. He rarely played golf.

After the jury selection, which took several hours, the judge read the indictment to the jurors. It appeared that the crux of the indictment was Brad exposing his son to the inclemency of the weather. At two o'clock on a Tuesday afternoon the judge allowed the trial to begin.

The district attorney called four witnesses: the assistant golf pro who was on duty the day of the incident; a second assistant pro who allowed Brad to borrow a cart to go talk to his son; one of the young boys who played with Darren that fateful day; the doctor who testified to the cause of Darren's death, which was being struck by lightning.

It appeared the most damaging testimony was that of the assistant pro who described the lightning sensor to Brad. He testified that Brad knew the sensor was activated because of lightning in the area. On that day he explained to Brad how the sensor operated. He testified that Brad became concerned and left to get his son. He said he was surprised when Brad returned to the clubhouse without his son.

On cross-examination by Brad's attorney the assistant pro acknowledged that very few golfers left the course when the sensor first sounded. He remembered that around the time Darren was struck by the lightning there were still several golfers playing the course. He gave the impression that the lightning appeared to be in the distance and not close to the golf course.

The only witness for the defense was Brad who was called to testify at one p.m. the following day. He testified that he believed the lightning was not a threat because it was so far away. At the time he went into the clubhouse he saw that most golfers remained on the course. If he believed for a moment that Darren was in danger he would not have let him remain on the course. While on the witness stand he paused several times to keep from crying. His attorney did not ask Brad a lot of questions but the prosecutor did.

The essence of the prosecution's questions was that Brad knew a danger existed or he would not have driven to warn his son. She made the point that if Brad had brought his son to the clubhouse he would be alive today. Brad's testimony ended at two-thirty.

During closing arguments the prosecutor's main argument was that Brad knew the danger existed or he would not have driven to his son. In spite of the danger Brad refused to protect the boy. She expressed her sympathy for Brad but argued that the jury in reaching a decision should not consider sympathy. Her final words were, "All Brad had to do was to take his son out of the inclement weather and that boy would be here today."

Brad's attorney argued that Brad acted like any other reasonable parent. He asked about the proximity of the lightning and was told that it was in a five miles radius. The dark clouds and lightning were not over the course when he checked the weather. Finally the attorney argued that Brad did not knowingly, intentionally or negligently expose his son to the inclemency of the weather.

Before the jury returned to their room to deliberate the judge gave them several instructions. The last instruction controlled the outcome of the case.

"For you to find Brad Howard guilty of child abuse resulting in death as charged in the indictment, the state must prove to your satisfaction beyond a reasonable doubt each of the following elements of the crime:

1. Brad Howard caused Darren Howard to be exposed to inclement weather.

2. The defendant acted with reckless disregard. To find that Brad Howard acted with reckless disregard, you must find that defendant knew or should have known the defendant's conduct created a substantial and foreseeable risk, the defendant disregarded that risk and the defendant was wholly indifferent to the

consequences of the conduct and to the welfare and safety of Darren Howard.

3. Brad Howard's failure to act resulted in the death of Darren Howard.

4. Darren Howard was under the age of eighteen."

The instructions the judge read to the jury were given to the jury to take with them to the jury room. They were allowed to refer to these instructions during their deliberations. It was four p.m.

It became divisive when the jury considered whether Brad acted with reckless disregard. Should he have taken his son into the clubhouse? Did Brad know that his conduct created a substantial and foreseeable risk? Was Brad wholly indifferent to the consequences of his conduct and to the welfare and safety of Darren?

The jury made its decision Friday afternoon at five p.m.

What is your verdict?

7

Manslaughter Without Pulling The Trigger

Two years past since Paul Miller met Janice Crist. When they met he was thirty-four and she was thirty. He was on the rebound from a marriage that ended in a bitter divorce. The first year they dated they seemed to have fallen deeply in love. Paul worked as a stockbroker and Janice worked as a bookkeeper for a construction firm.

During the second year of their relationship Janice began drinking an excessive amount of alcohol beverages. Sometimes Paul also engaged in excessive drinking. When they got drunk together they often fought.

On many occasions, both drunk and sober, Janice would tell Paul that she hated life and wanted to commit suicide. Paul insisted that she seek psychiatric help. She made one visit to the doctor who gave her a prescription for depression. Alcohol was not compatible with the medication and she used it sparingly. Her depression did not go away and she continued to threaten suicide.

Paul told her he would leave her if she did not take her medication and stop threatening suicide. She loved him and tried to do as he asked. For a couple of weeks it appeared that her behavior had changed. Then one Friday night things changed.

They went to dinner and both drank several alcoholic beverages. She became more intoxicated than Paul. They left the restaurant and went to Paul's townhouse. When they arrived she demanded one more drink. Paul told her she was too drunk and refused to give her another drink. She rushed to the bathroom and got one of Paul's razor blades. She told Paul she would slash her wrist if he did not let her have a drink.

Paul decided to see if she really meant it and refused to give her a drink. She began to cry, sat down on the couch and put down the razorblade. He felt that this showed that she really would not commit suicide.

One week passed without any problems between them. On another Friday night they went to a movie then stopped at a bar for a late night snack. Once again both of them drank excessively. Paul refused to drive his vehicle and they went to his townhouse in a taxi.

When they got there Janice immediately went to the cupboard, grabbed a bottle of vodka and made herself a drink. Paul sat at the kitchen table wanting to sober up. Janice sat at the table and began to talk about hating life and wishing she were dead She kept talking for about five minutes then Paul got up and went to his bedroom. He wanted to see if there was a way to stop her from talking about suicide. He reached under his mattress and got his loaded thirty-eight handgun. He went back to the room where Janice was still drinking. He intended to put the gun on the table and tell her that if she meant to commit suicide this was her chance. He believed she would react the same way she had with the razorblade.

When he put the gun on the table he said to her, "If you really mean it here's your chance." She grabbed the gun put it to her head and before he could respond, pulled the trigger and killed herself.

Paul immediately called 911. It took the police ten minutes to reach his townhouse. They questioned him about the event and he told them the exact truth. The officer in charge arrested him for the crime of manslaughter.

The indictment that formally came from the grand jury recited the statute in that state that Paul was accused of violating.

"Manslaughter

(a) A person commits an offense if he recklessly causes the death of an individual.

(b) An offense under this section is a felony of the second degree.

The penalty for a second-degree felony is not more than twenty years nor less than two years in prison."

The lawyer that Paul hired told him that this was a case of "first impression." This meant that no one had ever been charged with manslaughter for behavior like his. The lawyer believed he might be able to plea bargain for a lesser offense. He was wrong. The prosecutor wanted to go to trial and try to set a precedent.

Six months later the case went to trial. Before the attorneys questioned the potential jurors the judge read the indictment to them. The indictment specified the acts that were considered to have violated the state law. Some of the jurors appeared confused as the indictment was read.

After a lengthy eight-hour procedure the following jurors were selected to decide the defendant's fate: a fifty-year-old fed ex deliveryman with a twenty-nine-year-old daughter and a thirty-two-year-old son; a sixty-one-year-old retired dental assistant, mother of two daughters and two sons all over thirty-years of age; a thirty-two-year-old unmarried male real estate agent; a sixty-six-year-old retired high school principal father of five children the youngest being thirty years; a twenty-nine-year-old doctor's assistant, married and mother of a three-year-old girl; a thirty-six-year-old male stock broker, married with no children; a fifty-seven-year-old accountant, married and mother of a twenty-nine-year-old daughter; a fifty-year-old hairdresser, married and father of two girls twenty and twenty-three-years-old; a forty-two-year-old optometrist, married and father of a sixteen-year-old boy; a twenty-five-year-old unmarried female college student majoring in psychology; a thirty-seven-year-old plumber, married and father of a nine – year-old daughter; a thirty-nine-year-old electrician, divorced father of twin eleven-year- old daughters.

Opening statements commenced and the prosecutor presented his case. He attacked the defendant as a man who was drunk and acted recklessly and that such behavior was sufficient to convict Paul of manslaughter.

Paul's attorney defended Paul's behavior. He described Paul's behavior as a person trying to help a human being with a psychological problem. Unfortunately, because of Paul's lack of expertise he made the wrong decision, but his behavior was not a crime.

The witnesses for the prosecution were the doctor who declared the cause of death and the police officer who investigated the accident. The officer's testimony informed the jury about the admissions Paul made. The prosecutor's case took approximately three hours. Paul's lawyer did not cross-examine the prosecutor's witnesses.

Paul testified on his own behalf. He told the jury about Janice's prior act with the razorblade. He said he believed that she would respond the same way with the pistol and maybe stop the threatening acts. He didn't believe for a moment that she would shoot herself.

During cross-examination by the prosecution, Paul was asked why he did not take the bullets out of the gun. He responded that he thought about it but believed that Janice would see an empty gun and the effect on her behavior would not have been helpful to her. He said he thought he would have time to intervene. It was clear that Paul did not have any intent to harm Janice.

During closing arguments the prosecutor argued that intent was not an issue in the case. The issue was whether the defendant acted recklessly and whether his acts caused Janice's death. He told the jury that any person giving a gun to a person threatening suicide acted in a reckless manner and should be found guilty of manslaughter.

Paul's attorney told the jury that they must take all the circumstances under consideration when they decide if Paul's acts were reckless. He admitted that Paul made a mistake but that his error did not amount to recklessness. Paul tried to get her to quit threatening suicide for her own benefit. This was an act of concern that ended in a tragedy. He said that Paul should not be convicted of a felony for his mistake.

Following closing arguments the judge gave instructions to the jury. Here is the dominant instruction.

" For you to find the defendant guilty of manslaughter as charged the state must prove to your satisfaction beyond a reasonable doubt each of the following elements of the crime:

1. Paul Miller gave Jane Crist a handgun that she used to commit suicide.
2. Paul Miller should have known the danger involved by his actions.

3. Paul Miller acted recklessly.

4. Paul Miller's act caused the death of Janice Crist."

At eleven a.m. the jury went to the jury room to begin deliberations. They returned with their decision at five p.m.

What is your verdict?

8

Don't Give Beer To A Minor

In late August the parents of Judy Rich organized a party for her sixteenth
birthday. The party started at seven p.m. on a Friday evening. Several relatives and friends attended. Her seventeen-year-old brother Johnny was there with two of his friends who were eighteen-years-old.

Close to seven-thirty Johnny and his friends started drinking beer. There was only a six-pack available and it did not last very long. When the last beer was gone Johnny approached his uncle Bill Rich and asked him if he would go get them some more beer.

Bill who was forty-nine-years-old was divorced

and had a seventeen-year-old daughter who lived in another state. He owned a mechanical repair company, which he started ten years ago. In his spare time he helped coach a twelve-year-old boys soccer team.

Bill asked them how much they already consumed and they replied, two beers each. He checked the time. It was eight-thirty. He thought that getting them three more beers each would not create a problem. Bill told them that he would accommodate them if they agreed not to leave the premises without his permission. All the boys agreed. Bill and Johnny drove to the liquor store and Bill purchased nine cans of beer. When they returned to the party at nine o'clock, each one of the boys took a beer and began drinking.

At ten thirty all but one of the beers was gone. One of Johnny's friends took the last beer and began drinking. Johnny tried to snatch the beer and a struggling match ensued. Johnny began to make a lot of noise.

The next-door neighbor became upset at the noise and called the police. The police arrived within ten minutes. They approached the house and Johnny's father greeted them. Johnny was standing near his father and the police noticed that he appeared to be intoxicated. They went to Johnny and asked him if he had been drinking alcohol. When he responded affirmatively they asked him how much. He said he drank several beers. They asked him his age. He responded, "seventeen." They asked him who gave him the beer and he told them uncle Bill gave him the beer.

The police asked for Bill's whereabouts. Bill heard them and stepped forward. One officer asked Bill if he gave beer to Johnny and Bill answered affirmatively. The officer told Bill that because Johnny was less than eighteen Bill had contributed to the delinquency of a minor and that he was under arrest. Bill was handcuffed and taken to the police station. Several hours later he was released on bail.

Early the next morning Bill went to a criminal attorney's office. He discovered the applicable law that he was accused of violating. Contributing to the delinquency of a minor consists of any person committing any act or omitting the performance of any duty, which act or omission causes or tends to cause or encourage the delinquency of any person under the age of eighteen years. The attorney told him that giving beer to a minor under the conditions that existed at the party seemed to be exaggerating the law. He felt the district attorney would not submit this case to a grand jury. He was wrong. Three weeks after his arrest Bill was indicted.

Five months later thirty potential jurors were seated in the courtroom waiting to be questioned by the attorneys. The judge read the following state statute.

"Contributing to delinquency of a minor.

Contributing to the delinquency of a minor consists of any person committing any act or omitting the performance of any duty, which act or omission causes or tends to cause or encourage the delinquency of any person under the age of eighteen years.

Whoever commits contributing to the delinquency of a minor is guilty of a fourth degree felony."

A maximum sentence of eighteen months was the penalty for a fourth degree felony.

Here are the citizens selected by the attorneys to decide Bill's guilt or innocence. The first four jurors were women; a thirty-nine-year-old married mortgage loan officer who had two children, a sixteen-year-old daughter and a fourteen-year-old son; a fifty-two-year-old divorced insurance agent mother of a twenty-five-year-old daughter; a sixty -year-old married retired postal employee mother of two grown sons; a forty-seven-year- old married psychologist, mother of a twenty-year-old son and a sixteen-year-old daughter.

All the remaining jurors were men; a forty-four-year-old married restaurant owner, father of a seventeen-year-old son and a fourteen-year-old daughter; a twenty-six year-old unmarried stock broker; a twenty-three-year-old single college student who worked part time as a bartender; a sixty-three-year-old married real estate broker and father of four adult children; a thirty-two-year-old married grocery store manager, father of a three-year-old son and an eighteen-month-old daughter; a sixty-seven-year-old divorced retired fireman who had three adult children; a fifty-one-year-old married office manager for a utility company who had a twenty-one-year-old son and a nineteen-year -old daughter; a thirty-three-year old divorced federal express employee.

When jury selection was completed the judge told the jury that opening statements would begin at one p.m. that Tuesday afternoon.

At one p.m. the prosecutor gave his opening statement. His main point was that he would prove that the defendant assisted a minor in violating the law that prohibited anyone under the age of eighteen from drinking alcoholic beverages.

Bill's attorney told the jury that he would show that no delinquency on the part of any minor occurred the night Bill was arrested.

During the trial the prosecutor called only the

arresting police officer and Johnny as witnesses. He proved that Johnny was a minor under the age of eighteen and that Bill had bought beer for Johnny. The police officer read the law to the jury that prohibited anyone under the age of eighteen from drinking alcoholic beverages.

Bills' defense attorney had two witnesses, Johnny's father and Bill. Johnny's father testified that he permitted his son to drink beer while at home. He would not let his son leave the premises if he had a single beer. Bill testified that he got the boys to promise that they would not leave the premises without his permission. He wanted to make sure they did not leave the house if they were under the influence of alcohol.

The trial did not last very long. It ended at ten-thirty a.m. Wednesday morning.

Both attorneys closing arguments were short. The prosecutor argued he proved the defendant violated the law when he gave the beer to Johnny. He argued it did not matter that Johnny did not leave the premises. The gist of the crime was that the defendant caused Johnny to commit the offense of consuming alcohol while under the age of eighteen years.

The defense attorney argued to the jury that no delinquency occurred. He emphasized that Johnny's father permitted him to drink beer while at home. That is exactly where Johnny drank his beer. Johnny was in no position to commit any delinquent acts. Bill did not contribute to the delinquency of a minor.

When closing arguments ended the judge gave the jury several instructions. The instruction that controlled Bill's fate was the final instruction.

"For you to find the defendant guilty of contributing to the delinquency of a minor, the state must prove to your satisfaction beyond a reasonable doubt each of the following elements of the crime:

1. The defendant gave beer to a seventeen-year-old boy.
2. This encouraged the boy to consume alcohol and violate the state law, which does not permit a minor to drink alcoholic beverages.
3. Johnny Rich was under the age of eighteen."

The jury began deliberating at two o'clock. They returned with a verdict at four forty-five p.m.

What is your verdict?

9

Truck Owners Standard of Care

Two years had passed since John Maple bought his tractor and double log hauling trailers. He had enough work hauling logs for a timber company to make the truck payments and provide a good living for his wife and his twelve-year-old son. John was thirty-five years old and worked as a truck driver since he was twenty-six. He worked for a large company for seven years before he decided to try going out on his own.

John did not own a mechanical shop. Whenever the truck or trailers needed servicing he had an independent mechanical shop service his vehicle along with the trailers. He also inspected his truck on a regular basis.

Five days a week John would drive his car to the logging camp where his truck and trailers were parked so that the loggers could load logs onto the trailers. There were several other logging trucks at the same location. When his trailers were loaded he would drive the vehicle down a narrow dirt road. The dirt road was very bumpy and John drove his vehicle with great care and at a slow pace before reaching a paved highway that would lead him to a lumber mill. It was a fifty-mile drive to the lumber mill from the place where the dirt road ended. When he reached the lumber mill all the logs were unloaded. When the unloading was completed he would return to the logging camp and leave the truck and trailers to be loaded for the next day's trip.

In late August John took a one week vacation with his wife and son. During that week he left his truck at the mechanics shop where they serviced the vehicle. The trailers were left parked at the logging camp.

On the Monday morning the week after his vacation John got his truck from the mechanic shop and drove to the logging camp. When he arrived he conducted an inspection of the trailers. The trailers were loaded with logs. He connected the truck to the trailers and began his trip to the lumber mill.

At ten o'clock he reached the highway. As he drove down the highway he turned on the radio and listened to the news. Fifteen minutes passed when suddenly he heard a loud noise and felt his steering pulling hard to the right. He began to slow the truck and maintained a steady pace. He looked in his rearview mirror and saw logs falling off the rear trailer. The front trailer was under control. It took about three minutes for him to stop the truck and pull it to the side of the highway. He jumped out of the truck and ran to the rear trailer and saw that something broke under the trailer and caused the logs to spill onto the highway. He looked down the road behind him and saw that an automobile was hit by a couple of the logs. The automobile was on the side of the road about a quarter of a mile behind John.

He went to the cab of his truck and got his cellular phone. As he moved to the stricken automobile he dialed 911. He told the operator about the accident and she said she would have the police and an ambulance sent immediately.

When he got to the automobile he saw a man in the driver's seat, unconscious with his head covered with blood. John unsuccessfully tried to open the door Within twenty minutes the state police car arrived.

Shortly after the police arrived an ambulance came. The driver of the automobile was removed. He was dead.

The police performed an accident investigation. It was determined that an axle on the rear trailer broke. That was the cause of the accident. No citations were issued to John.

Sadness engulfed John even though he did not feel he was responsible for the accident. He believed, however, that there would be a civil claim against him. He notified his insurance company.

A month after the accident John received a telephone call from the district attorney's office. One of the assistants wanted a personal meeting with him. He told John that he could bring a lawyer with him if he wished. John told him he would come by himself.

The meeting between John and the assistant district attorney lasted for a half hour. Inspection of the trailer axles was the focus of the meeting. John did not have any records of the last time he had the axles checked. He thought they had been inspected within the last year and would try and find any records substantiating his belief.

After the meeting John could not find the records he needed. He reported his findings to the assistant district attorney. He asked the assistant if he was considering criminal charges against him. The assistant told John not to worry.

Three months later John received in the mail a grand jury indictment charging him with involuntary manslaughter. Immediately he called a criminal attorney whom he knew. A meeting was arranged for the next morning.

During the meeting the attorney telephoned the assistant district attorney who was assigned to the case. They talked for five minutes. After the conversation the attorney told John that his failure to regularly examine the axles amounted to a willful disregard for the safety of others. He told John that he might be able to negotiate some kind of plea bargain but also told John that he had a good chance of winning the case. They decided to proceed to trial.

Four months after the indictment the trial began on a Tuesday morning. The first action by the judge was to read the indictment and the state law to the potential jurors.

"Involuntary manslaughter consists of manslaughter committed in the commission of an unlawful act not amounting to a felony, or in the commission of a lawful act which might produce death in an unlawful manner or without due caution and circumspection.

Who ever commits involuntary manslaughter is guilty of a fourth degree felony."

Seven women and five men were selected as the jurors.

The women were: a forty-two-year-old married airline employee; a twenty-eight-year-old married mortgage loan officer; a sixty-one-year-old widowed secretary; a fifty-two-year-old female housewife whose husband was a truck driver; a sixty-five-year-old married and retired; a twenty-six-year-old college student who worked part time as a cocktail waitress; a forty-six-year-old married grade school teacher.

The five males consisted of a forty-two-year-old married electrician; fifty-two –year-old divorced police officer; a twenty-six-year-old single law student; a fifty-seven- year-old married restaurant owner; a thirty-nine year old married pharmacist.

At one o'clock p.m. the prosecutor began his opening statement. He emphasized that the cargo John hauled was totally different from the standard cargo in an enclosed trailer. He said he would prove that a log hauler had a higher standard of care when it came to inspecting the trailers and that John did not maintain the standard of care required of him. John's failure to exercise due caution caused the accident which resulted in the victim's death.

John's attorney told the jury that John did everything expected of a person who drove logging trucks. He would provide a witness who would testify that the flaw in the axle could not have been seen by the naked eye.

The main witness for the prosecution was an ex-vehicle inspector for the Department of Transportation. He testified that the inspections he conducted on logging trucks were more thorough than those inspections conducted on other types of trailers. The reason he gave was that a load that could be released to oncoming traffic was clearly more dangerous than the enclosed trailers. It was a matter of common sense.

The main witness for John's defense was an ex-supervisor for the Department of Transportation. He supervised the government inspectors. He agreed that inspections on logging trucks were more thorough. However, it was his expert opinion that a standard inspection required by the driver would not have discovered the flaw in the axle.

The case ended on Wednesday afternoon at two p.m. During closing arguments both attorneys emphasized the testimony of their expert witnesses.

The judge gave several instructions including the following.

"For you to find the defendant guilty of manslaughter, the state must prove to your satisfaction beyond a reasonable doubt each of the following elements of the crime.

1. John Maple drove his truck on the state highway and the trailers' axle broke and caused the logs on the trailer to fall and hit an oncoming vehicle and the driver of the vehicle was killed.

2. John Maple should have known of the danger involved by his actions.

3. John Maple acted without due caution and circumspection.

4. John Maple's action caused the death of Allen Wood."

The jury deliberated until five p.m. Since they had not reached a verdict the judge sent them home for the night. They returned at nine a.m. Thursday morning and deliberated until eleven o'clock when they reached their verdict.

What is your verdict?

10

Do We Punish A Poor and Under-privileged Mother?

Someone called the sheriff's office and reported that three children were left alone in an apartment. When the deputy arrived at the apartment he noticed a padlock on the outside door, which was the only way in or out of the home. He found three children inside the apartment, a boy fifteen years of age and two girls ages eight and five.

The boy told the officer that his mother locked the door when she went to work, from three to eleven p.m. He had a key for the lock but had to crawl out of the window to use it. There was no electricity in the apartment because the mother did not have the money to pay the electric bill. She hoped to use the week's pay to get the electricity on again. The father was in prison.

The part of town they lived in had pockets of gangs that might vandalize or burglarize any home or apartment. The mother was aware of the potential danger for her children.

The mother was promptly arrested on three counts of felony child abuse. A bond of fifteen thousand dollars was set, a sum she could not afford.

Josie Marquez, age thirty-four tried to care for her children the best way she could. She worked eight hours a day for low wages. She had fallen on hard times with her husband in prison. There was no electricity nor a working refrigerator. An icebox was used to keep things cold.

There were no signs that she ever abused the children. They were well fed and she took good care of them considering the difficult circumstances. She used all her restaurant pay to care for her children.

Having no money to pay an attorney, a public defender was appointed to defend Josie. She was accused of three third-degree felonies, very serious offenses.

Several months after the incident she was brought to trial in spite of some public outrage against her arrest and detention. It was a Wednesday morning when the judge read the indictment to the potential jurors. " The defendant has been charged with three counts of child abuse. Abuse of a child consists of a person knowingly, intentionally or negligently, and without justifiable cause, causing or permitting a child to be placed in a situation that may endanger the child's life or health."

The jury consisted of six men and six women. The male jurors consisted of a furniture salesman, age forty-two, married with a fifteen-year-old daughter and a twelve –year-old son; a used car sales manager, age thirty-nine, married with a son twelve-years- old; a retired railroad conductor, age sixty-eight, married with three adult children; a heavy equipment salesman, age thirty-two, single with no children; a high school teacher, age thirty-six, married with three daughters ages nine, seven and three; a construction engineer, age fifty, married with no children.

The female jurors were as follows: a masseuse, age thirty-three, divorced with no children; a secretary for a highway contractor, age fifty-nine, a widow with two adult children; a twenty-six-year-old medical student, unmarried with no children; a receptionist for brokerage firm, age thirty-seven, divorced with a twelve-year-old daughter; a forty-year-old housewife, mother of three children, a son age seventeen and two daughters, ages fourteen and twelve; a sixty-seven-year-old retired high school principal, widowed with two adult children and several grandchildren.

In his opening statement the prosecutor emphasized the fact that if a fire occurred the younger children's lives would be in jeopardy. This constituted negligence in permitting those children to be placed in a situation that endangered their lives.

The defense attorney told the jury that the acts of the defendant were prudent under the circumstances. She wanted to protect her children from burglars or any other attackers. She left a key for the padlock. Her son was fifteen and old enough to care for his younger siblings.

The main witnesses for the prosecution were the deputy and a social worker for the state Children, Youth and Family Department. They emphasized the padlock and the lack of electricity as being the main negligence endangering the lives of the children.

One witness was called by the defense, Josie. She testified that the electricity was off because she did not earn enough money to pay the last bill but planned to use her next paycheck to have the electricity turned back on. The padlock was on the door to discourage anyone from breaking in and attacking her children. She also testified that her children were well fed and very healthy. She believed her fifteen-year-old son was mature enough to deal with most emergencies.

The trial ended Thursday at three-thirty p.m. The judge gave the instructions including the following critical instruction.

"Josie Marquez has been charged with negligently permitting child abuse. For you to find the defendant guilty of child abuse the state must prove to your satisfaction beyond a reasonable doubt each of the following elements of the crime.

1. Defendant permitted her three children to be placed in a situation, which endangered their lives.

2. The defendant acted with reckless disregard and without justifiable cause. To find that defendant acted with reckless disregard, you must find that defendant knew or should have known that defendant's actions created a substantial and foreseeable risk, the defendant disregarded the risk and the defendant was

wholly indifferent to the consequences of her actions and to the welfare and safety of the children.

3. All three children were under the age of eighteen."

Only an hour remained before the judge would allow the jury to go home for the evening. To everyone's surprise, before the hour was over, the jury notified the judge they had reached a decision.

What is your verdict?

The Jury Verdicts

1.

A sad-appearing foreman read the verdict to the court, guilty as charged. When Leslie took the child on the street while wearing roller blades the jury believed that the child was placed in a situation, which endangered its life. They were also convinced that Leslie acted with reckless disregard and that she should have known of the risk and disregarded that risk.

2.

In this case the jury believed that Alex's use of his cellular phone constituted operating a vehicle in a reckless manner. It also was convinced that a semi-truck driver is showing willful disregard of the safety of others when using a cellular telephone. The verdict was guilty.

3.

Having two rottweilers was a substantial and un-justifiable risk that a result would occur. The risk was of such a nature that Ursula's failure to perceive it con-stituted a gross deviation form the standard of care that a reasonable person would exercise under all the cir-cumstances. The jury returned a verdict of guilty.

4.

A failure to see a decimal point in a doctor's or-ders was not the type of conduct that met the substan-tial and unjustifiable risk that was stated in the instruc-tion. The jury did not believe Julie deviated from the standard of care. It was just a bad accident. Not guilty.

5.

There was no question that Dale caused the dog's injury but the jury did not accept that Dale's acts were intentional. Not guilty.

6.

Reasonable doubt in two main areas existed in the charges against Brad Howard. It was not Brad who exposed the child to the inclement weather and Brad's behavior was not reckless. Not guilty.

7.

All the jurors agreed that Paul Miller did not act intentionally but they agreed that he acted recklessly and his act caused the death of Janice Crist. They found him guilty.

8.

There was no question that Bill Rich gave beer to a minor. The jury believed that by obtaining liquor for the minor the defendant encouraged the minor to consume alcohol. Therefore, they found the defendant guilty.

9.

Due caution and circumspection were the deciding factors in this case. The jurors did not accept the prosecution's argument that John Maple acted without due caution and circumspection. Not guilty.

10.

All the jurors felt Josie Marquez should not have been charged with any crime. Their lives were not in danger and she did not act with reckless disregard. Not guilty

www.ingramcontent.com/pod-product-compliance
Lightning Source LLC
Chambersburg PA
CBHW012011190326
41520CB00025B/7509